TEN WORDS,
TWO SIGNS,
ONE PRAYER

11-3-14

Ben & Carolyn,

Thanks so much for
your faithful support
of Asbury Seminary!

Many Blessings,

Jay Endicott

TEN WORDS,
TWO SIGNS,
ONE PRAYER

Core Practices of the Christian Faith

Timothy C. Tennent

Printed in the United States of America

Library of Congress Control Number: 2013951026

Hard Cover ISBN: 978-1-62824-066-5
Paperback ISBN: 978-1-62824-067-2
Mobi ISBN: 978-1-62824-068-9
ePub ISBN: 978-1-62824-069-6
uPDF ISBN: 978-1-62824-070-2

Cover design by Haley Hill

Page design by Haley Hill and Kristin Goble

SEEDBED PUBLISHING
Sowing for a Great Awakening
204 N. Lexington Avenue, Wilmore, Kentucky 40390
www.seedbed.com

To John and Ellen Nicodemus who have demonstrated through their lives and witness the rhythms of faith and practice that we long to see throughout the church.

Contents

Introduction xi

Part I: The Ten Commandments

Introduction: The Ten Commandments and
the Moral Code of the Old Testament 5

Commandment 1 .... *You Shall Have No Other* 15
                      Gods Before Me

Commandment 2 .... *You Shall Not Make for* 21
                      Yourself an Idol

Commandment 3 ..... *You Shall Not Misuse the Name* 29
                      of the Lord *Your God*

Commandment 4 .... *Remember the Sabbath Day* 35
                      by Keeping It Holy

Commandment 5 .... *Honor Your Father* 43
                      and Your Mother

Commandment 6 .... *You Shall Not Murder* 51

Commandment 7 ..... *You Shall Not Commit Adultery* 57

Commandment 8 .... *You Shall Not Steal* 65

Commandment 9 .. *You Shall Not Give False Testimony* 69

Commandment 10 .... *You Shall Not Covet* 75

Part II: Two Sacraments: Baptism and the Lord's Supper

Introduction 85

Baptism 89

The Lord's Supper (Communion) 101

Part III: The Lord's Prayer

Introduction 115

Petition 1 .... *Our Father in heaven, hallowed be your name* 121

Petition 2 .... *Your kingdom come, your will be done* 127
                        on earth as it is in heaven

Petition 3 .... *Give us today our daily bread* 133

Petition 4 .... *Forgive us our debts, as we also* 137
                        have forgiven our debtors

Petition 5 .... *And lead us not into temptation,* 143
                        but deliver us from the evil one

Final Thoughts 153

Notes 155

About the Author 159

Introduction

Catechesis, or the oral instruction that a new Christian receives, is sometimes wrongly understood as only focused on the key doctrines or beliefs of the church. However, while it is true that it is essential that the church protect itself against false teachings and preserve the apostolic witness, this is not the sole function of catechesis. Historic catechesis has always been like a three-legged stool; the loss of any part results in the collapse of the whole. The three "legs" of catechesis are *doctrine, holiness,* and *practice.* In other words, the church has not been satisfied that the faith has been "passed on" until the new believer is shaped and formed in what he or she believes (doctrine), how he or she lives (moral/holiness), and what he or she practices (spiritual disciplines).

A survey of catechesis over the centuries shows a remarkable agreement that the core doctrines of the church are best captured in the Apostles' Creed; the core moral or holiness code is best captured in the Ten Commandments; and the core spiritual disciplines are best captured in the Lord's Prayer and the sacraments. Thus, a common outline for catechesis would look something like this:

Apostolic doctrine:	"What the church believes"	Apostles' Creed
Christian holiness:	"How the church lives"	Ten Commandments
Spiritual disciplines:	"Core practices of the church"	Lord's Prayer/ sacraments

This book is a sequel to two previous publications entitled *This We Believe!* and *Thirty Questions*. In *This We Believe!* I dedicated a chapter to a simple, straightforward explanation of each phrase of the Apostles' Creed. It is being used by churches around the country (and, indeed, all over the world, as it has now been translated into several languages) to assist in the catechesis of the church.

In *Thirty Questions*, I looked at the top thirty questions that every Christian should be able to answer. This book also comes with an explanation that answers each of the thirty questions so that parents or Sunday school teachers can easily use this guide to instruct and to train new Christians in the faith. It is in question-and-answer format because not only has this traditionally been a common catechetical device, but it naturally builds on the innate curiosity children have that leads them to ask questions. Both of these previous books can be obtained through amazon.com or seedbed.com.

This little book, *Ten Words, Two Signs, One Prayer*, is the third and final installment in this catechesis series. It focuses on the Ten Commandments, two sacraments: baptism and the Lord's Supper, and the Lord's Prayer, thereby completing the last two legs of the stool.

TEN WORDS,
TWO SIGNS,
ONE PRAYER

PART I

The Ten Commandments

Introduction: The Ten Commandments and the Moral Code of the Old Testament

The Ten Commandments appear twice in the Old Testament. The first time they appear is when the Israelites have been delivered out of centuries of slavery and brought through the Red Sea. One of the early stops in their wilderness wanderings was Mount Sinai (also called Mount Horeb). It was there that Moses received the Ten Commandments from God.

The Ten Commandments appear a second time in the Old Testament in Deuteronomy 5. By this time, a whole new generation stands before Moses, as the previous generation had died in the wilderness because of their unbelief and rebellion against God. Moses is at the end of his life, and the book of Deuteronomy contains five final sermons Moses gives to the people before he dies. The Israelites are all gathered on the plains of Moab and listening to Moses restate the law a second time. This is why the book is called *Deuteronomy*, a word that means "Second Law," meaning the Law is being repeated a second time. Thus, in Deuteronomy 5, the Ten Commandments are repeated, as is much of the legislation that appeared earlier in Leviticus.

When Moses originally received the Law from God, it took place on Mount Sinai. Moses ascended the mountain and received the Law through a series of revelations from God over a forty-day period. We do not know precisely how these laws came to Moses, but the New Testament indicates (and it was widely taught in Judaism) that the Law was given to Moses through the mediation of angels (Acts 7:53; Gal. 3:19). However, something dramatic happened with the Ten Commandments. These commands were given directly by God to Moses and were actually written on two tablets of stone by the very "finger" of God. Exodus 31:18 says that "he [God] gave to Moses, when he had finished speaking with him on Mount Sinai, the two tablets of the testimony, tablets of stone, written with the finger of God" (ESV).

These commands are actually called the Ten Commandments in several passages of Scripture, including Exodus 34:28, Deuteronomy 4:13, and Deuteronomy 10:4. The phrase can also be translated "Ten Words," and frequently the Ten Commandments are referred to by Jewish and Christian teachers as the Decalogue, which means the "Ten Words."

Traditionally, Jewish rabbis, dating back to a third-century rabbi named Simlai, have identified 613 distinct laws that appear in the Old Testament. Rabbi Simlai identified 248 of these as "positive commands," namely, commands for us to do something. For example, Leviticus 19:36 commanded the Israelites to use just measurements and weights. It was common at that time for people to sell food in the market by weight. Some merchants would secretly cheat people by using weights that were below the standard weight. This command showed God's interest in promoting integrity in the marketplace.

Three hundred sixty-five of the commands were "prohibition commands," telling God's people to avoid certain things. For example, Leviticus 19:14 commanded them not to put an obstacle in front of a blind man, demonstrating God's special kindness toward those with special needs.

The 365 "thou shalt nots" and the 248 "thou shalts" add up to the overall number of 613. So, if there are 613 laws, what makes the Ten Commandments so special, and why were they given to us in such a dramatic fashion?

The Ten Commandments are broad, summative commands. This means that all of the 613 laws of the Old Testament will, in one way or another, find their fulfillment and logical expression in one of the ten. Thus, the Ten Commandments are a wonderful way for someone to understand the heart of the Law. They are not simply a set of negative commands. Rather, the Ten Commandments represent the pathway out of our own self-orientation and into a whole new orientation that puts God, ourselves, and others in their rightful places.

It has been observed that of the 613 laws, only 77 of the positive commands and 194 of the negative commands apply today because quite a few of the laws relate to specific actions around the temple (which no longer exists) and the particular practices related to Israelite worship (which no longer apply to the church). Yet, even those commands, if examined closely, reflect deeper moral concerns of God which find their broad expression in the Ten Commandments. Thus, the Ten Commandments are not bound by any particular time, culture, or covenant. They reflect a timeless moral code that is applicable to all people everywhere. For this reason, the Ten Commandments have been found at the core of Christian catechesis manuals for centuries.

Occasionally some modern Christians will object to any emphasis on the Law on the grounds that we are saved by grace and are, therefore, free from the Law. They sometimes cite Galatians 3:24–25, where Paul says, "So the law was put in charge to lead us to Christ that we might be justified by faith. Now that faith has come, we are no longer under the supervision of the law." The modern objection is based on several misunderstandings, which can easily be cleared up.

First of all, it is important to understand that this passage is referring to justification, not salvation. Justification is the initial act of being set right with God. This is like the entrance, or doorway, into the Christian faith. It is absolutely true that no amount of law keeping can ever enable someone to enter heaven or earn salvation through works. The Bible makes this clear in many passages, including Romans 3:24, which says that we are "justified freely by his grace through the redemption that came by Christ Jesus."

However, salvation is a much bigger concept than justification. When we are forgiven for all of our sins, God no longer sees our sins, but He sees the righteousness of Jesus Christ. This is, of course, the good news of the gospel. However, this is an alien righteousness. In other words, it is a righteousness belonging to Christ, not to us. Thus, justification is followed by sanctification, where we are actually made righteous. John Wesley called this "going on to perfection." (Christians disagree about how much progress toward righteousness is possible in this life, but all agree on the importance of living righteously.)

Second, it is through sanctification that our lives are formed and shaped by holiness. It is not to earn our justification; it is to grow in the grace and knowledge of Christ, and become transformed more and more into His likeness. There are dozens of passages that call us to a holy life. For example, 1 Peter calls us to "not conform to the evil desires you had when you lived in ignorance," but instead, we are to "be holy" (1:14–16). Paul declares that "it is God's will that you should be sanctified . . . for God did not call us to be impure, but to live a holy life" (1 Thess. 4:3, 7). The writer of Hebrews tells us that "without holiness no one will see the Lord" (Heb. 12:14).

When Paul wrote in Galatians 3:25 that we were "no longer under the supervision of the law," it should not be understood that we are free from the moral Law of God. What it means is that the Law was incapable of making us holy, so we needed a better supervisor than a mere command. In short, we need more than a command to make us holy; we need the tutelage of Christ. So Christ is now our new and better "supervisor." He is our mentor, our guide, our example, and our champion in holiness. Through the power of the Holy Spirit, God can transform us in ways that the Law never dreamed of.

But the point is that Christ now enables us to truly become holy, not that Christ's redemption somehow frees us from all moral obligations and we can live however we want to because we have been "saved by grace." Paul himself condemns this attitude when he says, "Shall we go on sinning so that grace may increase? By no means! We died to sin; how can we live in it any longer? (Rom. 6:1–2). In short, we should never, ever confuse justification with salvation, any more than we should confuse the front door of a house for the entire house.

In fact, even justification and sanctification are not the full picture of salvation. Scripture teaches that even after we die we will receive a final glorification whereby we will be fully transformed into Christ's likeness in even deeper and more profound ways than our sanctification here can accomplish. So, *salvation* is actually a very broad term that encompasses justification, sanctification, and final glorification.

The Ten Commandments, therefore, remain the best summary of God's moral code. They are our initial tutelage into the life of holiness. The presence and power of Christ not only enable us to keep these Ten Commandments, but empower us for the deeper obedience to which these laws ultimately point. The chapters that follow will take each of the commands one by one and give a brief exposition as to what it means and how it may apply to our twenty-first-century context.

COMMANDMENT 1

You Shall Have No Other Gods Before Me

This first command, found in Exodus 20:3, stands at the head of the Ten Commandments. It begins in a way that, for some, may seem surprising. One normally thinks about moral commands as relating to our relationship one with another. If the Decalogue had begun with commands such as, "Do not steal," or, "Do not lie," and so forth, it would have sounded a lot like an array of moral codes ranging from the Eightfold Path of Buddhism to the Egyptian code of Ma'at to the Babylonian Code of Hammurabi. All of these ancient codes regulate a whole range of outward behavior, from purchasing property, to settling disputes between people, to divorce, but they do not reference any moral obligation toward God. The Ten Commandments, conversely, build all morality on the foundation of our moral obligation toward God. This reinforces the fact that, biblically speaking, there is no such thing as morality that is not theological. In other words, all morality in our relationships must be first rooted in a right relationship with God.

The first commandment calls us to have no other gods before Him. This command reaches far deeper than merely closing the door on an atheistic worldview. Just because you do not deny the existence of God does not mean that you have kept this commandment. Even if you affirm that God loves you and is the source of your redemption, you may not have fully kept this command. The first commandment is about the whole orientation of our lives. It means the end of a compartmentalized life that gives God a certain portion (like Sunday morning) and then orients the rest of our lives around our own perceived needs and goals.

The New Testament demonstrates the direction of this first command when Jesus Himself is asked, "Which is the greatest commandment?" Jesus replies by saying, "You shall love the Lord your God with all your heart, and with all your soul, and with all your mind. This is the great and first commandment. And a second is like it: You shall love your neighbor as yourself. On these two commandments depend all the Law and the Prophets" (Matt. 22:36–40 esv).

No study of the Ten Commandments would be complete without a reflection on this teaching of Jesus. I have already pointed out that the Ten Commandments are a grand summary of the 613 laws of the Old Testament. In the New Testament, Jesus summarizes the Ten Commandments even further, as all fall under two general headings: (1) Love God and (2) Love your neighbor. Jesus' words in Matthew are clearly a summary of the Ten Commandments, since they are divided into these two general areas. The first four commandments deal with loving God (no other gods before Me, no idols, do not misuse the name of the Lord your God, and remember the Sabbath Day) and the last six focus on loving your neighbor (honor your father and mother, do not murder, do not commit adultery, do not steal, do not give false testimony, and do not covet).

When Jesus is asked, "What is the greatest commandment?" He begins by saying, "You shall love the Lord your God with all your heart and with all your soul and with all your mind. This is the great and first commandment" (vv. 37–38 ESV). Notice that Jesus calls this the "great" and the "first" commandment. It is not just an allusion to the first part of the Ten Commandments (commandments 1–4), but in particular, an exposition of the first of the Ten Commandments. The way we have no other gods before us is to have our whole orientation around the true and living God. We obey this command by loving God with all our hearts, souls, and minds! This means that the whole focus of our lives is on Him. It encompasses our hearts, our minds, our whole strength and will.

Jesus Himself gives us the greatest exposition of the first commandment. His use of words like "heart," "soul," and "mind" gives us in seed form the full range of human life and activity. When Jesus says we are to love God with our whole hearts, He is not referring primarily to an emotional or privatized love in the way this term is often used to describe our devotion to God. It, of course, does not exclude this. Jesus actually points us to a deeper reality. The first commandment encompasses all of our active energies, our minds, and indeed, the whole orientation of our lives before God. When we roll up our sleeves to serve the poor, we are loving God. When we read the Scriptures and think about the ways of God, we are loving God. When we share our faith with others, we are loving God. The first commandment does not merely happen during a Sunday morning worship service or in our daily times of prayer and devotion. The first commandment is the active God-ward orientation of our whole lives throughout the day. This is the commandment that enables us to "pray without ceasing" (1 Thess. 5:17 ESV). It is also the commandment that enables us to not pass the wounded traveler by.

The first commandment is the foundation for our keeping of the whole of the Ten Commandments. It is the most basic reorientation from a life directed toward ourselves to a life directed toward God. Therefore, we should view this first commandment as the doorway into the whole life of faith. It sets our feet on the right path and orients us in the right direction for all that follows.

COMMANDMENT 2

You Shall Not Make for Yourself an Idol

The second command, probably more than any of the Ten Commandments, seems rather remote to many contemporary Christians living in the Western world. This commandment, on the surface, focuses specifically on the prohibition of idolatry. The primary manifestation of idolatry in the ancient world was in the making of idols and the use of them in various acts of worship. In the context of the ancient world, an idol refers to any man-made material object used to represent God. The prohibition against idolatry appears throughout the Old Testament.

The second commandment specifically prohibits making an idol "in the form of anything in heaven above or on the earth beneath or in the waters below" (Exod. 20:4). This command is designed to eliminate all impulses to make idols of the stars or planets, or of any creature on the earth, whether in the sky or on land or in the sea. Other places in the

Old Testament mention specific materials that were apparently used in idol making. For example, in Leviticus 19:4 Moses said, "Do not turn to idols or make gods of cast metal for yourselves." The casting of metal, especially in the ancient world, was an old but specialized technology. The shaping of idols was widespread, and Israel had to be warned against it. Another part of Leviticus makes reference to idols carved from stone: "Do not make idols or set up an image or a sacred stone for yourselves, and do not place a carved stone in your land to bow down before it. I am the LORD your God" (26:1).

In reflecting on the second commandment, we should be wary of two potential dangers. The first is the assumption that idol worship and the kind of idol making described in the texts above was only to be found in the distant ancient world. The second is the assumption that given the absence of literal idol making and idol worship in our society, the second commandment is no longer relevant for contemporary Christians today.

Let's examine both of these assumptions. Over the last twenty-five years, I have traveled to India every year to teach at New Theological College (NTC), a training school located in the mountains of North India, close to the Ganges river and at the heart of the Hindu religion. Over the years I have seen hundreds of idols of various gods and goddesses, especially Shiva and various incarnations of Vishnu, such as Rama and Krishna. They can be found, quite literally, in Hindu temples in every corner of the country, as well as in Hindu homes and various public places. Some of these idols are massive figures that tower over an entire city and were built with great sacrifice and effort. Others are small idols that can be found on a shelf in a home or in someone's business. Hindus living in the twenty-first century are, therefore, unaware that idol making and worshipping various forms of graven images is an offense to God's holiness.

It is important to remember that the Bible is for all peoples in all cultures, and this particular command in its original form and force is just as applicable to Hindus (as well as other religious groups in the world) as it was to the Israelites when it was first given. We should also not underestimate the presence of physical idols in all parts of the world. Due to the rise of global migrations, as well as the growing fascination with Eastern religions, idols can now be found all over the world. Hindu and Buddhist temples are being built across the Western world, and they are becoming increasingly common.

As to the second assumption, we should not think that we have "kept" the commandment by merely avoiding the kind of outward idolatry that we might associate with popular forms of Hinduism. The second commandment would apply to anything we put in the place of God. In the contemporary world the word *idol* is used to describe any person or thing that we greatly admire. Many people think of certain film stars as "idols," and everyone knows the popularity of the singing competition show *American Idol*, which has launched the careers of many rising singers by making them "idols." This is an example from popular culture, but it does underscore how an idol can be anything we set up in the place of God. It could be a person, a job, a salary, a position, a title, or a secret sin, to name just a few examples.

You see, there is nothing inherently wrong with a piece of carved wood, a chiseled stone, or a cast of metal. We all have various items in our homes that have been carved from wood or are made from a cast of metal. We do not need to destroy these items out of a fear that we have violated the second commandment. Something—indeed, *any* thing—becomes idolatrous when we falsely impose on it a place and a dignity it does not deserve. That is the essence of all idolatry, whether in the Late Bronze–Early Iron Age of the biblical period or in twenty-first-century America.

The prophet Isaiah powerfully demonstrates the true nature of idolatry in the forty-fourth chapter of his prophecy. He describes an idol maker who takes a cypress tree and cuts it down. With one part of the trunk, he cuts a piece of firewood and uses it to keep warm or to bake bread. With the other part of the trunk, he fashions an idol and then bows down to it and worships it, saying, "Save me! You are my god!" The prophet then points out how ridiculous this is. He says, "No one stops to think, . . . 'Half of it I used for fuel; I even baked bread over its coals,'" and with the other half, "'I [made] a detestable thing'" and "'bow[ed] down to a block of wood'" (Isa. 44:13–19).

In the same way, two people may be side by side, doing similar jobs in the same company. One person views his or her job as an opportunity to use his or her gifts in service to the Lord. For the other person, though, the job has become an idol, or "like a god" to him or her. In both cases the job provides sustenance, security, and a sense of purpose. The first employee in our example sees this as a gift from God and knows that ultimately his or her sustenance, security, and sense of purpose comes from God alone. The second employee has put the job itself, rather than God, in this position. This is the nature of all idolatry. Thus, the second command calls us to examine ourselves and to honestly ask ourselves what or in whom do we trust?

Is there anyone or anything on the throne of your life other than God Himself? Pope Francis recently commented on idolatry, saying, "Idols exist . . . as a pretext for setting ourselves at the center of reality and worshiping the work of our own hands."[1]

There is another way in which idolatry manifests itself. For some of us, we may never have worshipped any physical idol, and we may truly believe that God is on the throne of our lives. Yet, we have a distorted and false conception of God that we have put in His place. Sometimes a distorted view of

God Himself can become an idol, if we replace the true and living God with a god more in keeping with our own imaginations. We may have placed a god without judgment—or a god without grace—on the throne. The second commandment calls us to worship the true and living God, who has revealed Himself in Scripture and ultimately in Jesus Christ. He alone do we worship, and to Him alone we bow down.

COMMANDMENT 3

You Shall Not Misuse the Name of the LORD *Your God*

What does it mean to "misuse" the name of the Lord (Exod. 20:7)? This cannot be properly answered without first understanding the importance of someone's name in the biblical material. We often choose names based on how they sound, or because of some family connection, without much consideration for the deeper meaning. However, in the ancient world names were chosen with meanings that reflected the character of the father or mother, or certain anticipated character traits for the child. So, for example, though the name Abimelech is just an odd name to us, in Hebrew it means "my father is king," thereby reflecting something about the child's father. The name Hannah means "favor" or "grace," and the name Benjamin means "son of the right hand," both indicative of circumstances surrounding the child's birth or, possibly, qualities hoped

23

for in the life of the child. The point is that biblical names are closely identified with one's character.

We all know that circumstances can cause someone to change his or her name to reflect a new situation. Abram (meaning "exalted father") became Abraham ("father of nations"). In the New Testament, Jesus gives Simon the name Peter (Greek) or Cephas (Aramaic), which means "rock." In the book of Revelation we are promised that God is going to give to each of those who overcome "a white stone with a new name written on the stone." (2:17)

To invoke someone's name meant to call upon the character of that name and the power associated with it. So, when we say, "Bless His holy name," or we pray, "Our Father which art in heaven, hallowed be your name" (Matt. 6:9 KJV), we are acknowledging the holiness and the sacredness of His name. To "call upon the name of the Lord" is to invoke all the power and character associated with that name. This is why the Lord is given so many different names in the Bible, such as Savior, King of kings, Everlasting Father, Chief Shepherd, Comforter, Wonderful Counselor, high priest, light of the world, Prince of Peace, Redeemer, Lamb of God, the true vine, and so forth (see Isaiah 9:6; 45:21; 53; 63:16; John 1:29; 8:12; 14:26 KJV; 15:1; 1 Timothy 6:15; Hebrews 2:17; 1 Peter 5:4). In short, a name in the Bible is not merely a useful appendage to help facilitate one's identity. Rather, it is linked with the whole of the character and the very essence of the person.

To "misuse" God's name, therefore, involves a whole range of ways in which we do not show proper respect or reverence for the character and power of God. To use God's name in profanity is an obvious example. But, like the other commandments we have examined, it is too easy to distance ourselves from the force of the command by giving ourselves the false assurance that we have "kept" the commandment simply because we do not use God's name in some profane expression or vile oath. This command also extends to all the myriad of ways we invoke God's name in casual and, sometimes, flippant ways. This happens in the relaxed talk among Christians who are quick to invoke God's name, attributing our certain knowledge of what God thinks about this or that situation, whether political, religious, or in the sporting world. We misuse God's name when we allow songs or choruses that diminish the majesty and character of God to be used for worship.

To "misuse" God's name also involves things we may not readily recognize as a violation of the third commandment. Christianity is not merely a private matter. To be a Christian is to be invited as a Christian into the whole of life. We work as Christians. We play as Christians. We shop as Christians. We marry as Christians. We think as Christians. We watch films as Christians. There is no part of our lives that is exempt from the lordship of Jesus Christ. We are, in essence, bearers of the name of Christ in the whole of life. This means that His reputation has been bound up with ours.

This is a sobering thought. It means that when we do things or live in ways that are dishonoring to God, we bring shame and disrepute to the name of Christ. Likewise, when we demonstrate extraordinary patience or sacrificial love or faithful service, we bring honor to the name of Christ. The early church, when persecuted, rejoiced that they had been counted worthy to "suffer . . . for the name" (Acts 5:41). So, keeping the third commandment means living our whole lives in ways which bring honor and glory to His Name.

COMMANDMENT 4

Remember the Sabbath Day by Keeping It Holy

The Sabbath Day does not begin with the Ten Commandments (Exod. 20:7), but is interwoven into the very fabric of creation itself. At the very dawn of creation, God established the Sabbath. In fact, it is the creation account in Genesis that defines our week—six days of creation, and the seventh the Sabbath day. The seven-day week does not come from the natural order (as do the month and the year), but emerges out of the creation account in Genesis 1 and 2.

The Bible teaches that God is the author of all creation. We are not given exact details on the process or timing, but we know that God is the author of all creation, and that the creation account is organized around a seven-day week. In the first six days God created the entire world, and on the seventh day God rested.

The word for "rest" used in Genesis 2:2 is where we get our word *sabbath*. It means "to cease," or "to rest." The use of the word "rest" could not possibly mean that God was exhausted after creating the world. It is impossible for God to be tired or to need rest. The whole of creation emerges through His creative, spoken word and does not tax the infinite energy or resources of the Divine Majesty! Rather, the word is used to indicate that God "ceased" from His labors that He might dwell on and enjoy a creation of His own making that He has called "very good" (Gen. 1:31).

Unlike the other six days of creation, which all came to an end, the seventh day was not meant to end. All of creation was meant to live in the ongoing "Sabbath" of God. It was the entrance of sin into the world, through the disobedience of Adam, that brought the Sabbath to an end. The Sabbath was not so much a *day* as a *condition*—a time to cease and to celebrate God's rule. When Adam and Eve rebelled against God's rule and reign, they broke the Sabbath because they shattered the ongoing celebration of God's rule, which was meant to be the undergirding foundation of the productivity that came forth from the Garden of Eden.

With this background in mind, we are better able to look at the fourth commandment. I have already pointed out that the Ten Commandments are found in two places in the Old Testament. There are only minor variations in the two versions, but one of the differences relating to the fourth commandment is worth noting. The actual wording of the fourth commandment is identical in Exodus 20 and

Deuteronomy 5, but the *reason* given for the commandment is different. In Exodus 20 the Sabbath is rooted back into the creation account and, therefore, is meant as God's gift to the whole human race, both believers and unbelievers. It is part of God's design that all people have a healthy rhythm of work and rest in life. In contrast, Deuteronomy 5 roots the Sabbath legislation into a specific response to Israel's deliverance from Egyptian slavery. This reflection will focus on what the Sabbath specifically means for us as Christians, though an equal treatment could be given for Sabbath as a general gift to all people everywhere.

There are three important points about the Sabbath that are significant for Christians to hear from this text. First, the Sabbath is not just about our *not* doing something. It is not simply about inactivity. That is the problem Jesus encountered with the Pharisees in the New Testament who had made the Sabbath into a legalism of "not doing." Instead, the fourth commandment calls us to *remember* the Sabbath day to *keep it holy*.

Moses was not establishing something new, but rather calling us to remember what once was. It is a weekly reminder that the world today is not as it should be, that we have all been broken by the Fall. We long for the day when God's Sabbath reign will be reestablished in the New Creation at the end of time (Rev. 21–22). We honor the Sabbath and keep it holy by remembering what the world was like before we shattered it through sin. We cease from our labors so that we can remember why we work the other six days and recognize that the most important things that happen in our lives are the things that happen through *God's* work.

Second, the Sabbath is our weekly opportunity to break our trust in work. Jesus had conflict with the Pharisees because they had turned their inactivity on the Sabbath into another form of "work" so that they could establish their own self-righteousness. Jesus makes it clear that the Sabbath is not an obligation that we grudgingly undertake to make God happy. The Sabbath rest is God's gift to us. This is why Jesus said, "The Sabbath was made for man, not man for the Sabbath" (Mark 2:27). We've turned the Sabbath into a law of inactivity. It is vital that we cease from our labors every week, but that ceasing in and of itself is not what constitutes Sabbath. Rather, it is a day to quit trusting in our works and allow God to work.

The reason we cease from our labors one day of the week is because we need to take time to remember. It is a weekly reminder of our dependence on God. For most of us, our work gives us three things: our self-worth, our sustenance, and our sense of independence. The Sabbath reminds us that our self-worth comes first and foremost from God, that He is our Provider and Sustainer, and that we are totally dependent upon Him. Breaking our weekly trust in work actually enables us to work better and more effectively the other six days because it is now kept in the proper perspective.

Third, the Sabbath is a celebration of the resurrection and the future reestablishment of the Sabbath. In the Old Testament, the fourth commandment looked backwards at the original creation and how God ceased His work on the seventh day. In the New Testament, the Christians wisely shifted the focus from the seventh day to the first day of the week, which was the day of the resurrection of Christ. By doing this, they were looking forward to Christ's second coming and the New Creation, when the Sabbath reign of God will be reestablished.

We no longer look back and remember what should have been; instead, we look forward and eagerly await the new heavens and the new earth. In Christ, we see the in-breaking of these future realities and a foretaste of the health and wholeness and full reign of the kingdom that is to come. Dedicating a day once per week for worship, rest, reflection, and renewal is but a tiny foretaste of the final Sabbath rest that will be reinstituted once Christ has returned and sin has been banished. All of life will be "Sabbath," not a ceasing from work, but work without drudgery, and in the complete absence of sin, in the fullness of God's fruitful design.

COMMANDMENT 5

Honor Your Father and Your Mother

The family is the most basic unit of community. It is designed by God to be the building block of a healthy society. In fact, the family is meant to be a reflection of the triune God Himself. In God's very triune nature, we find relationship, mutual edification, nurture, beauty, creativity, and love in full perfection. The family is designed to reflect something of God's life into the world.

It is, therefore, no surprise that at the heart of the Ten Commandments—the fifth commandment—we find a commandment designed to protect and support the family unit. It is here that the Ten Commandments move from a focus on our lives before God (commandments 1-4) to a focus on our relationship with one another (commandments 5-10). This is important because it is a tangible demonstration that our spiritual and moral formation is not limited to our relationship with God, i.e., our justification. Rather, it is also intimately connected to our relationship with one another, that is, our sanctification. We can be justified by ourselves bowing at an altar before God, but we cannot be sanctified that way. Sanctification takes place in community, in the context of our relationships. Thus, the last six commandments of the Ten Commandments rightly extend our formation to include all of our other relationships.

Before we even begin to examine the specific force of the fifth commandment, it is important to recognize three underlying assumptions that undergird this command.

First, the command assumes the reproductive fruitfulness of married life. In other words, married people will normally have children. A "family" is assumed to be a mother, a father, and one or more children. We are, of course, aware of many examples where married people are unable to have children. This calls for our compassion and special understanding, but, from the biblical perspective, it would never be regarded as normative, or a "choice" that was comparable to married life with children.

Occasionally, modern Christians have objected to the church's participation in Mother's Day or Father's Day on the grounds that it may be a source of pain for those who are single or who may not have been able to have children. But a close reading of the text makes clear that this command is written from the perspective of a child who is called to honor his or her mother and father. Every person on earth has a mother and a father. Whether you are still single or not is irrelevant because the command is to honor *your* mother and father. The same applies to a woman who is, as yet, unable to give birth. The command does not say, "Honor your father-hood," or, "Honor your motherhood," but "Honor *your* father and *your* mother" (Exod. 20:12, emphasis added).

Second, the command assumes the presence of a father and a mother in the home. Today, a growing percentage of children are growing up in homes that have been fractured through separation and divorce. This is a call for the church to do a better job helping young people build strong, sustainable families. The church is often silent on practices that have been destructive to family life, even while it has a responsibility to help single parents to rebuild their family life. Surrogate and adoptive parents or grandparents can step into a broken home and provide the support and love that are needed.

Third, the commandment assumes that marriage is between a man and a woman. Today, the very nature of marriage itself is in danger of being lost. We are losing the notion that there is a divine design to marriage. A covenantal view of marriage has gradually been replaced by the commodification of marriage, which finds its center, not in the triune God, but in the locus of the personal pursuit of happiness. This dynamic will be explored in more detail when we examine the seventh commandment.

Most of today's presenting problems (same-sex marriage, adultery, pornographic additions, and so on) are actually rooted in the shift from a covenantal view of marriage to marriage as a utilitarian commodity that functions for the purpose of our personal fulfillment. Since the church has unwittingly accepted the wider culture's view of marriage, we have very little room to maneuver. Once a functionalistic, commodity-driven, utilitarian view of marriage is accepted, then there really is no solid ground to stand on in opposing a whole range of new kinds of relationships that might be called "marriage."

The fifth commandment calls for us to resist the prevailing presupposition of a utilitarian, consumer view of marriage. In contrast, the Ten Commandments root family life into a covenantal view, designed by God, which goes back to creation itself. It is no mistake that the fifth commandment is known in the New Testament as the "first commandment with a promise" (Eph. 6:1–3). Paul admonishes children to honor and obey their parents and observes that this is the only one of the Ten Commandments that is connected to a promise of God's special blessing if you observe this command.

To honor your father and mother does not mean that their decisions and guidance are always right. Rather, we are called to honor them because they are in a place or a position that is highly honored by God. To honor your parents means to respect them. It means to show deference to their views, even while, as we get older and we become parents, we are increasingly able to interact with them almost as peers. At whatever age, we still honor and respect our parents. We defend them. We listen to them. We seek out their wisdom and counsel. In the process, we are laying the groundwork for our own success as parents and we help to extend the fruitfulness and efficacy of the marriage covenant to the next generation.

The fifth commandment also provides the basis for a whole culture of honor and respect. Since the family unit is the building block of a healthy society and nation, the fifth commandment establishes the broad basis for respect that is necessary for effective leadership. So, although this command begins with the smallest child, it extends outward to embrace the whole of society and provides the framework for the entire nation. A nation with children who do not honor their parents is a nation that will not honor God. Thus, the fifth commandment provides the proper foundation for the entire society.

COMMANDMENT 6

You Shall Not Murder[1]

It is important to recognize that the sixth commandment specifically focuses on murder. It does not say, "You shall not kill," but, "You shall not murder." The Bible recognizes certain situations where the taking of human life is justified. The Old Testament acknowledges twenty-six different offenses where the taking of life is allowed. Many of these involve ceremonial offenses, which are no longer applicable today. Others are specifically related to moral issues and involve, in several examples, offenses that we would classify today as "capital crimes." For example, Genesis 9:6 says that if someone "sheds man's blood, by man his blood shall be shed" (NKJV). This is an example of what we would call "capital punishment" in response to someone who murders an innocent person.

On the other hand, there are examples of capital crimes in the Scriptures that would not be recognized as such by today's society, for example, if someone worked on the Sabbath Day or persistently dishonored his or her parents (Num. 15:32–36; Deut. 21:18–21). The reason modern Western law does not legislate these kinds of commands is because we are not a theocratic state. Contemporary Western law does not require people to be religious, nor is it comfortable adjudicating motivations that have not borne fruit in specific acts against one's neighbor.

While complete pacifism has been a minority position within the church, there are many Christians throughout history who believe strongly that Jesus' admonitions to "love your enemies" (Matt. 5:44) and "turn the other cheek" (See Matthew 5:39) demonstrate a deeper ethic that overturns all forms of capital punishment. Others insist that this applies to personal relationships and does not apply to the state, which, according to Romans 13, continues to be "an agent of wrath to bring punishment on the wrongdoer" (v. 4).

Despite the differences on these points, however, all are agreed that the Bible clearly teaches that it is wrong to murder. Jesus, in particular, reaffirms this command (Matt. 19:18; Mark 10:19; Luke 18:20), and Paul specifically condemns murder in Romans 1:29 and 1 Timothy 1:9. Similar warnings can be found in the writings of James, Peter, and John (James 2:11; 1 Peter 4:15; 1 John 3:12–15). In fact, the New Testament assumes that the Christian command to "love your neighbor" is the greatest summary of the commandments "Do not commit adultery," "Do not murder," "Do not steal," and "Do not covet" (Rom. 13:9).

Murder is generally defined as the unlawful, premeditated killing of one person by another. The Bible, as well as our modern legal system, makes an important distinction between murder and manslaughter. The latter refers to a death that occurs unintentionally. The Old Testament provided special cities of refuge for someone "who kills a person accidentally and unintentionally" (Josh. 20:3). The person was instructed to stay there until he or she could stand trial and until the death of the high priest. After that, a person guilty of manslaughter could return to his or her hometown and resume normal life.

It is clear that the Old Testament provides a nuanced and reflective response to a whole range of human situations. Today, we are experiencing special challenges at the two ends of life: namely, abortion and euthanasia. The Scriptures acknowledge that life begins from the moment of conception and continues until the moment of death. David wrote, "For you created my inmost being; you knit me together in my mother's womb" (Ps. 139:13; see also Job 10:11–12). Likewise, God is sovereign over death: "The LORD brings death and makes alive; he brings down to the grave and raises up" (1 Sam. 2:6). Thus, the termination of pregnancies and active measures undertaken medically to prematurely end life would both be regarded as violations of the sixth commandment.

Jesus not only affirms the command, but deepens it by teaching that even if a person has not physically murdered someone, the command is broken when we hate someone in our hearts (Matt. 5:21–22). Therefore, Jesus acknowledges that this command has force for all of us in the way we interact one with another. In short, the force of this command is to acknowledge the sanctity of human life, the sacredness of human relationships, and the fact that God alone is the author of life.

COMMANDMENT 7

You Shall Not Commit Adultery

We have already seen in the fifth commandment the intentionality with which God protects the family unit. Two of the Ten Commandments are dedicated to this end. The fifth commandment is written from the perspective of the child. The seventh, located in Exodus 20:14, is written from the perspective of the person who has entered into the covenant of marriage.

"You shall not commit adultery." First, what constitutes adultery? Adultery refers to any form of sexual intercourse (oral, anal, coitus, etc.) between a married person and a person who is not his or her spouse. The command also, by implication, would prohibit all forms of fornication, including all sexual activity between any persons who are not married.

At the very threshold of this command we come face-to-face with a very distinctive biblical view of marriage, which must be understood if the commandment is to carry its proper force. Marriage is rooted in the very fabric of creation itself. God created man and woman and brought them together into a "one flesh" relationship (Gen. 2:24). Marriage is part of a divine design and is therefore an institution rooted in His triune life. It does not arise later as a utilitarian function of human life and society.

As noted earlier in our discussion about the fifth commandment, this has huge implications for today. In place of a divine design, there is a popular understanding that has been widely embraced (even within the church). The popular narrative is as follows: Marriage is a way to find personal fulfillment and happiness. Marriage is defined, so the narrative goes, as a legal arrangement that allows two people to fulfill each other's emotional and sexual needs and desires. Individual freedom, personal autonomy, and personal fulfillment are very high values in the West, and marriage has been domesticated to fit within that larger utilitarian framework. Today we stay connected to people only as long as they are meeting our particular needs at an acceptable cost to us. When we cease to make a profit—that is, when the relationship appears to require more love and affirmation from us than we are getting back—then we "cut our losses" and drop the relationship. This is known as the "commodification" of marriage, a process by which social relationships are reduced to measurable economic and emotional exchange units.

With this framework, marriage is fully privatized, taking it out of the public sphere completely. Its purpose is redefined as individual gratification and happiness, not any "broader good." There is no place for things like sustaining the race, reflecting God's nature, producing character, raising children, reflecting the triune God, becoming cocreators with Him, etc. Slowly but surely, this newer understanding of the meaning of marriage has displaced the older one in Western culture.

In Mark 10:1–12 the Pharisees seek to trap Jesus by putting a wedge between Jesus and Moses. They ask in verse 2, "Is it lawful for a man to divorce his wife?"

Jesus instantly recognizes the trap, and so He takes the initiative by asking in verse 3, "What did Moses command you?"

They tell Him in verse 4 that Moses permitted a man to write a certificate of divorce and send her away. This is a reference to Deuteronomy 24:1-4. A careful read of Deuteronomy 24, however, reveals that Moses did not actually command that men give their wives a certificate of divorce if they are displeased with them, as the Pharisees claimed. What you find is a series of four "if" clauses: *If* a man marries a woman who becomes displeasing to him because of something indecent, and *if* he writes her a certificate of divorce, and *if* after she leaves his house she becomes the wife of another and *if* her second husband writes her a certificate of divorce, or *if* he dies—*then* (and here is the legislation) her first husband is not allowed to marry her again. The legislation is actually intended to resist the easy dissolution of marriage, not to allow a man to casually dissolve his marriage with a certificate.

However, rather than focus on their faulty exegesis of a particular text, Jesus recognizes that the issue raised by the Pharisees is but a presenting issue of a deeper malady. This is why we have the reply, "It was because your hearts were hard that Moses wrote you this law . . . But at the beginning of creation God 'made them male and female'" (Mark 10:5-6). Jesus brings us back to creation. He understands that there are times when you have to go back to the beginning to get things set right. Even though His hearers were not actually interested in God's teaching on marriage, and were only trying to use this presenting issue to trap Him, He nevertheless proceeds to give us the greatest single teaching on marriage in the entire Bible, which is the most cited text in marriage liturgies in every Christian tradition: "At the beginning of creation 'God made them male and female. For this reason, a man will leave his mother and father and be united to his wife, and the two will become one flesh.' So they are no longer two, but one. Therefore what God has joined together, let man not separate" (Mark 10: 6-9).

We live in a time when the teaching of Jesus on marriage is mostly incomprehensible to the wider culture. The seventh commandment calls us anew to stop and recognize all of the various ways in which the whole array of sexual brokenness in our society has distorted God's original design of marriage. Indeed, it is precisely because we understand God's design for marriage that we can develop important pastoral responses to people who have experienced broken marriages. It also allows us to discover extravagant ways to show our love to homosexuals, or divorced people, or people who have escaped abusive situations, and so forth. The Bible acknowledges certain situations when divorce is permitted: most notably, when one spouse has been sexually unfaithful and therefore has already broken the covenant (Matt. 5:32), or in situations where an unbelieving spouse has abandoned or deserted a believing spouse (1 Cor. 7:15).

As we noted with the commandment regarding murder, Jesus also deepens the seventh commandment by teaching that even if we have not physically committed adultery, we nevertheless commit adultery in our hearts when we look with lust at another (Matt. 5:27–28). Thus, it is not merely the physical act of adultery that is cited, but any act—including the use of pornography—that is a violation of the seventh commandment. Thus, the underlying principle in the entire Bible is to uphold and protect the institution of marriage in the most solemn terms.

COMMANDMENT 8

You Shall Not Steal

The eighth commandment, on the surface, is about the protection of personal property. Theft is defined, broadly, as the unlawful taking of something that belongs to someone else. However, if you have ever been robbed, either by personal assault or by theft in your home, you will know that when this occurs, we feel personally violated and vulnerable in ways that are difficult to describe to those who have never been a victim of theft. In short, it is not merely about protecting personal property; it is about providing the basis for a just society, where people feel safe and secure.

Think of how much energy we expend in protecting our homes and computers with locks and security systems. Today, there are few acts that create more sense of vulnerability than for someone to steal your identity and make unlawful use of your credit cards, or to ransack your home, where once you felt safe and secure. All of these fears and vulnerabilities would melt away if the eighth commandment were honored and kept.

As with the other commandments, we should recognize that the eighth commandment has implications broader than what might appear on the surface. This command is not limited to the protection of our personal property. The eighth commandment, found in Exodus 20:15, prohibits all forms of stealing. This means, for example, that we have not "kept" the eighth commandment when we steal time from our employer by engaging in personal affairs rather than the work we have been paid to do. It prohibits stealing someone's ideas or "intellectual property," which is the basis for copyright laws or other measures society uses to protect all that belongs to another. When a student plagiarizes someone else's ideas without giving appropriate credit, we rightly regard this as a form of stealing. If we steal someone else's wife, then it is a violation of both the seventh and the eighth commandments. To murder is to steal someone's life, thereby violating both the sixth and the eighth commandments. To rape someone is to steal his or her virtue, and to rob the victim of his or her dignity. In short, there are many ways in which we can engage in theft which transcend the narrow bounds of personal property alone. All of this is captured in the eighth commandment.

Another area we do not often regard as stealing is in the area of tithes and offerings made to God. In the book of Malachi,

God regards holding back our tithes as an act of "robbing God" (3:8). In the New Testament, Ananias and Sapphira were under no obligation to sell their property and give it to the church. But once they made the pledge, and then withheld a portion for themselves, yet gave it under the pretense that it was the entire amount, they were struck down by God and died because of their deception (Acts 5:1–10).

It is, therefore, evident that the eighth commandment is designed not merely to curb shoplifting, but to protect honesty and integrity in the whole of our lives. As with all the commandments, to steal is not merely a crime against a person, but is ultimately an act against God, who is the author of the whole moral order, which He established as a reflection of His own character and image.

COMMANDMENT 9

You Shall Not Give False Testimony

We all know the familiar words used when someone stands before a judge and jury with his or her right hand raised and the officer says: "Do you solemnly swear to tell the truth, the whole truth, and nothing but the truth, so help you God?"[1] This is a very carefully worded legal statement designed to stop not only lying, but also deception and "half-truths." That famous legal phrase finds its origin in the ninth commandment, which establishes the moral basis for absolute truthfulness in all our statements, whether written or verbal. It is found in Exodus 20:16.

As Christians, we do not need to raise our right hands and be placed "under oath" to be compelled to speak truthfully. Rather, we live our whole lives, public or private, under the ninth commandment, which carries immeasurably more force than any court of law. The ninth commandment might be best understood as a bright, searing light. The light is so bright that it is able to dispel the darkness from even the most elusive corners and shadows. Let's take a look at some of these layers exposed by this light.

The first, most obvious, way to keep this commandment is by not lying. To lie is to intentionally give a false statement about someone or something that we know to be false. This is sometimes called a "bald-faced" lie. It is done intentionally and knowingly. There are times when we unknowingly state something that we think is true, but is, in fact, false. For example, occasionally someone will say that even after a person is dead, his or her fingernails and hair will continue to grow for a period of time. This is a factually false statement, but it would not be considered a lie since the person truly believed it to be true.

There are also times when people lie about matters that seem small because they do not involve someone else's life or reputation. This is sometimes called a "white lie," which refers to a statement that, though still a lie, is socially permitted. However, there is no allowance in the ninth commandment for any kind of lie. All of the Ten Commandments are rooted in God's character, and therefore, any breach, even a small one, impugns God's character and reputation.

The second layer that is exposed by the ninth commandment is deceptions or so-called half-truths. In this case, the statement may contain some element of truth, but for the purpose of misleading someone, the complete picture is not given. For example, take the case of a police officer who stops a swerving car, approaches the inebriated driver, and asks if he has been drinking. If the driver responds by saying, "I have only had two beers," it could be a technically factual statement. But if the driver had actually consumed two beers and several pints of vodka, then his statement was a half-truth intended to deceive. There are many examples in politics and in the world of advertising where half-truths are used to lead the hearer to a conclusion that may not be warranted if all the facts were known. This is why the courtroom oath includes the phrase "the whole truth." All such withholding of truth, or adding any deceptive statements, are forms of "giving false testimony," or "bear[ing] false witness," as the King James Version puts it.

The third layer exposed by the ninth commandment is keeping silent when our silence either leads someone to a false conclusion, or gives an impression that is false. There are certain situations where someone's life or reputation is at stake, and we have information that could lead to his or her exoneration or at least clarify a misperception. If we withhold that information by keeping silent, it is a violation of the ninth commandment. This third layer has many practical applications. One of the social maxims we have all heard is the phrase, "Silence is consent." It is a very ancient principle, but was made famous in the sixteenth century by Sir Thomas More, who used this defense in his interaction with King Henry VIII. Formally, the maxim is *"Qui tacet consentiret"* (Silence gives consent).

If you place a dozen plastic pink flamingos in your front yard, and no one complains, then it is commonly accepted that this implies that your neighbors are granting consent to the presence of plastic flamingos in their neighborhood. This widely accepted principle serves to heighten the implication of silence in Western culture. In fact, this principle has given rise to a number of well-known sayings such as, "Silence speaks louder than words," or, "Silence can be like the thunder," and so forth.

Thus, if you are standing around the water cooler at work and someone makes a false or misleading statement about your employer or one of your coworkers and you don't speak up, but just listen in silence, there is an implied acceptance of the statement. It requires courage and honest candor to speak up in these situations and, in the process, separate yourself from any tacit complicity in bearing false witness against your neighbor.

Like a searing light, the ninth commandment shines into our lives and calls us to the highest standards of truth and integrity. We live our whole lives under the moral mandate to tell the truth, the whole truth, and nothing but the truth, remembering the words of Jesus: "There is nothing concealed that will not be disclosed, or hidden that will not be made known. What you have said in the dark will be heard in the daylight, and what you have whispered in the ear in the inner rooms will be proclaimed from the roofs" (Luke 12:2–3).

COMMANDMENT 10

You Shall Not Covet

To covet something is to crave or to have an inordinate desire for something you do not have. The tenth commandment says, "You shall not covet." While all of the commandments, as we have seen, have various layers of application, the range of this command is broadly reviewed within the text itself. Exodus 20:17 says, "You shall not covet your neighbor's house. You shall not covet your neighbor's wife, or his manservant or maidservant, his ox or donkey, or anything that belongs to your neighbor."

In reading the full command, it might be easy for a modern reader to get distracted by what appears to be human commodification: namely, a possible interpretation that a "wife" is just another part of a man's property or, possibly, that this text is an implied endorsement of slavery. Neither is the case, as other Scriptures make plain. The point of this passage, although its original setting does arise out of the ancient world, is to highlight various things that distinguish people from one another. Perhaps in the ancient world having five servants would set you apart from your neighbor, whereas today it is that you drive a BMW and have a house on the lake. The point is that we compare ourselves with others and we develop inordinate, unhealthy desires for that which we do not have.

One of the most striking things about this commandment is that it does not focus on any outward activity at all. It is fitting that the tenth commandment brings the moral code of God right into the human heart. Hebrews 4:12–13 says that "the word of God is living and active. Sharper than any double-edged sword . . . it judges the thoughts and attitudes of the heart. Nothing in all creation is hidden from God's sight. Everything is uncovered and laid bare before the eyes of him to whom we must give account." This is where the Ten Commandments bring us. We are now looking at intentions and inner motivations.

It should be clear that there is nothing wrong with setting goals and working hard toward an academic degree, the purchase of a home, or a promotion at work. The idea that all desires are evil and wrong is a teaching of Buddhism, not of Christianity. The tenth commandment focuses on an *unhealthy* coveting of what belongs to another, and for which we are not prepared to work hard and earn, or for which we work for the wrong motivations. If our motivation is self-focused, or even if it is to earn God's favor (which cannot be earned), then we can easily find ourselves in violation of the tenth commandment. Comparing ourselves with others and wanting something or someone we don't have can give birth to coveting. Whether it is a possession, a position, or a person, we must keep ourselves free from such inordinate desires.

The Scriptures teach, "Keep your lives free from the love of money and be content with what you have" (Heb. 13:5). What a great liberation would be ours if we lived in such contentment! Jesus said, "It is more blessed to give than to receive" (Acts 20:35). The very idea that it is better to give what we have to others, rather than to covet for ourselves what someone else possesses, is a radical reorientation of an entire worldview that can so easily become dominated by worldly values rather than the values of the kingdom of God. Indeed, the tenth commandment represents a reorientation of our lives around the values of contentment, recognizing the needs of those less fortunate than ourselves, and drawing our identity and self-worth from God. It returns us to that reorientation of life and heart that the Decalogue pronounced in the opening command. This is the great gift that is ours if we keep the tenth commandment.

Conclusion

The Ten Commandments, or Decalogue, represent the broad outlines of a moral life that reflects the nature and character of God. The whole point of the Ten Commandments is not to merely establish rules of conduct, but to invite us into the joyful communion of God's presence, where moral and ethical stability abound, and through which we reflect His character and glory into the world.

The love of God is not some ephemeral emotional attachment God has for us. God's love is rooted in and expressed through a solid moral framework. The Decalogue invites us into His divine life. In short, it is not about them; it is about Him. It is His life we are entering, not a code inscribed on tablets of stone, or put on a poster board in a Sunday school classroom.

As we enter His life, we realize that all of the outward guidelines are but pointers to deeper heart issues: It is not just about murder; it is also about anger against our neighbor. It is even deeper than not being angry with our neighbor. It is being enabled and empowered to love our enemies and pray for those who persecute us. It is about more than prohibiting the act of adultery. It is realizing that we men commit adultery when we look at a woman with lust in our hearts. Likewise, women must realize that they commit adultery when they look lustfully at a man. But the gospel takes us even deeper, showing women how to respect their husbands, and showing we men how to love our wives as Christ loved the church. It is not just about not coveting; it is about learning to be a joyful giver. It is to these deeper realities that Jesus pointed in the Sermon on the Mount.

In the New Testament the Law was not being abolished, but fulfilled and revealed in its fullest glory to the church.

As we walk down this moral road, we begin to realize that it is finally about nothing less than the full rule and reign of God breaking into our lives and into this world. The New Creation is longing to dawn on the dark and broken world we inhabit and to which we so tenaciously cling. Yet, we cannot let go of this old order by ourselves. We can only embrace the in-breaking kingdom and the dawning of the New Creation when we are abiding in the life of Christ and empowered and enabled by the indwelling presence and power of the Holy Spirit. It is the triune God who alone will lead us into the fullness of joy that eagerly awaits us all. This is seldom better stated than in the following lines commonly attributed to John Bunyan:

Run, [run,] run, the law commands
But gives us neither feet nor hands,

Far better news the gospel brings:
It bids us fly and gives us wings.[1]

PART II

*Two Sacraments:
Baptism and the Lord's Supper*

Introduction

When a person has been released from prison or rescued from some dire condition, the first thing he or she needs to receive is a nice, warm bath and a meal. These are universal symbols of grace and hospitality. To receive someone into your home and offer him or her a bath and a meal is one of the surest signs of full acceptance and a real relationship.

This is, essentially, what God does with us after we are rescued from the bondage of sin, brought out of our imprisonment to Satan and into a new life in Christ. Our first act is to receive baptism, which is the Christian way of giving a new believer a "spiritual bath." This act simultaneously symbolizes both our cleansing from sin as well as a tangible reenactment of a death and resurrection. As we symbolically reenact Christ's own death and resurrection, we "die" to our sins and are raised to new life with Christ. Likewise, Communion, or the Lord's Supper, is the place where we sit down at a table in the presence of Jesus Christ, who serves as host, and we enjoy a meal together.

In the early church the Lord's Supper was not merely the tiny tokens of bread and wine that we have today. Rather, it was a full meal, known as the "love feast," which culminated in the symbolic eating of Christ's body and drinking of His blood as a way of declaring that we are united with Him in His death and resurrection. Today, Communion has been separated from the larger meal, so we may not fully recognize it as a "meal" with Jesus Christ, who spiritually stands at the head of the table as the host.

Jesus instituted these two ongoing practices of baptism and the Lord's Supper in the church as a way of marking out the new life in Christ. These are public, visible "signs" that point to Jesus Christ and the wonderful mysteries of redemption. These two practices are normally known as *sacraments*, meaning "sacred rituals," because Jesus Himself instituted them and commanded us to observe them. A *sacrament* has been defined as "an outward and visible sign of an inward and spiritual grace."[1] This means that it is a means of grace whereby God is truly present at the waters of baptism and at the Table, and *He acts* in the lives of those who come to the waters of baptism and the Lord's Supper.

Certainly, the grace of God and how He conveys that grace to us is a central theme of the Scriptures. The phrase "means of grace" is a general way of seeking to capture all of the ways God has appointed to convey His grace to men and women. Baptism and the Lord's Supper are the best examples of this. We will now examine each of the sacraments.

Baptism

As the risen Lord, Jesus Christ commanded His followers to "go and make disciples of all nations, baptizing them in the name of the Father and of the Son and of the Holy Spirit" (Matt. 28:19; see also Mark 16:16). The book of Acts gives ample testimony that this is exactly what the disciples did. For example, Acts records the first public sermon of the church on the day of Pentecost. In this sermon, Peter called for a response to his message with the following words: "Repent and be baptized, every one of you, in the name of Jesus Christ for the forgiveness of sins. And you will receive the gift of the Holy Spirit" (Acts 2:38). Throughout the Acts of the Apostles, we see that baptism is regarded as the public act of our repentance and the public transfer of a new believer from the kingdom of darkness into the kingdom of God.

In the New Testament, it is not sufficient to simply pray a sinner's prayer and be privately justified before God. Christianity, as the redeemed community, is to be a public witness before the world. In short, we are not only saved as individuals, but we are saved into a new community, known as the church of Jesus Christ. Baptism is the public sign of this transfer and should be the normal "first step" expectation of all new believers.[1]

Meaning of Water in the Scriptures

Why are new Christians asked to engage with water in such a public fashion? In the Scriptures, water has four main purposes/meanings, all of which are symbolically represented in Christian baptism. First, water is used around the world for cleansing. When a Christian undergoes baptism, it is an outward sign of the inward spiritual cleansing that has taken place through the gospel. In the Old Testament, priests were required to cleanse themselves with water before entering into the presence of God. (See, for example, Numbers 19:1–8.) In the same way, the waters of baptism symbolize the spiritual cleansing that is necessary to enter into the presence of a holy God.

Second, water is a symbol of the Holy Spirit. In John 7, Jesus declared, "Whoever believes in me, as the Scripture has said, 'Out of his heart will flow rivers of living water.' Now this he said about the Spirit, whom those who believed in him were to receive, for as yet the Spirit had not been given, because Jesus was not yet glorified (vv. 38–39 ESV). The association of water and the Spirit is another profound mystery. When Jesus Himself was baptized, the Holy Spirit came upon him in a special way (Matt. 3:16; Mark 1:9–10;

Luke 3:21–22; John 1:31–32). So, the waters of baptism symbolize the presence and infilling of the Holy Spirit in the life of the new believer. The apostle Paul teaches that "in one Spirit we were all baptized into one body—Jews or Greeks, slaves or free—and all were made to drink of one Spirit" (1 Cor. 12:13 ESV).

Third, water is a symbol of birth. At the time of our physical birth, the first sign of new life is the "breaking of water" that accompanies the new birth. We are born "out of water" into the world. In the same way, the presence of water symbolizes that a new, spiritual birth has taken place and we are being brought into the world as a new creation. Jesus told Nicodemus that no one could see the kingdom of God unless he was "born of water and the Spirit" (John 3:5). Nicodemus was amazed because he thought that Jesus was saying we must somehow reenter the womb and be born a second time. However, Jesus was using an analogy, comparing our spiritual birth with our first physical birth.

Finally, water is used to symbolize our death to sin and our resurrection to new life. There is no real connection between water and burial, but when we go down into the waters of baptism and then emerge from the water, it is symbolic of our being buried with Christ, and then rising to new life. Paul asks, "Do you not know that all of us who have been baptized into Christ Jesus were baptized into his death? We were buried therefore with him by baptism into death, in order that, just as Christ was raised from the dead by the glory of the Father, we too might walk in newness of life" (Rom. 6:3–4 ESV).

Mode and Formula of Baptism

The church has different practices regarding the precise method to be used in baptizing someone and what formula, if any, should be employed. Broadly speaking, there are three modes of baptism that are practiced in the church around the world: sprinkling, pouring (or effusion) over the head, and total immersion in water. All three modes embrace all four of the above meanings of baptism, but some emphasize one more than others. Total immersion is the most widely accepted mode since it so obviously captures the "death and burial" theme noted above. Sprinkling or pouring draws upon the Old Testament practice of sprinkling water and blood on the sacrifices. In the prophecy of Ezekiel, God says, "I will sprinkle clean water on you, and you shall be clean from all your uncleannesses, and from your idols I will cleanse you. And I will give you a new heart, and a new spirit I will put within you. And I will remove the heart of stone from your flesh and give you a heart of flesh" (Ezek. 36:25–26 ESV). In the early church sometimes sprinkling was used because of the infirmity of the candidate or, quite practically, because of the scarcity of water in the desert regions.

As long as the meaning and symbolism are made clear, the precise mode should not be a point of division in the church, since the New Testament does not clearly specify the mode. Christians should remember that meaning trumps mode. Therefore, we should be gracious with other Christians who were baptized by a different mode than the one we experienced, as long as the public, spiritual transfer has taken place.

When someone is baptized, it is the instruction of Jesus Himself that they be baptized in the name of the triune God (Matt. 28:19). This means that when people are baptized, they should be asked if they have repented of their sins and have trusted Christ for their salvation. Some traditions also ask candidates if they will renounce the devil and all his works. Upon assent, they are baptized "in the name of the Father, the Son, and the Holy Spirit." When people are baptized "in the name of Jesus" only (as occurs in the book of Acts), it is generally understood that the "name of Jesus" is representative of the triune God, since you are baptized by the redemptive act of God the Father, in the name of Jesus, and through the power of the Holy Spirit.

Who should be baptized?

The more crucial question concerns not the precise mode, but clarity on who is eligible for baptism. Almost every Christian tradition agrees that an unbaptized believer who comes to Jesus Christ should be baptized.[2]

The point of serious disagreement concerns whether an infant is eligible to be baptized before he or she even has an opportunity to personally repent and believe. Those traditions (such as Baptist, Anabaptist, and Pentecostal) that emphasize the importance of personal repentance and conversion prior to baptism insist that it is wrong to baptize an infant. Since infants cannot repent and believe, they are, therefore, not eligible for baptism, according to these Christians. Therefore, the sacrament should be reserved until a person is prepared to confess his or her own sins and confess Jesus Christ as Lord and Savior. This is a solid position, and Christians who come from different traditions (like Roman Catholics, Orthodox, Presbyterians, Lutherans, Anglicans, and Methodists) should respect and appreciate the biblical and theological reasons given for this position.

However, there are other Christians who insist that the focus on a believer's baptism tends to obscure the corporate, community nature of baptism. In other words, baptism is more than simply a sign of one's personal justification before God. Baptism is an act of being brought into the family of God. In this view, children of believing parents are joyfully welcomed into the church family. Baptism signifies their "belonging" to the family of God. In the Old Testament, infants were circumcised as an "outward sign" of their membership in the Jewish covenant. In the same way, baptism is an outward sign of our belonging to the family of God.

Later, when children reach an age of being able to make their own decision for Christ, they are asked to go through a confirmation class, where they publicly declare that they "confirm" their infant baptism. It is, therefore, not correct to say that those who practice infant baptism are not interested in an adult, public profession of Christ. Rather, the baptism is permitted at the earliest age, and then it is later united with a formal confirmation class and public profession of faith. This view has a more covenantal view of baptism. That is, it focuses on the community nature of the people of God, which later is confirmed by an individual, public decision. Jesus was very welcoming of children, and even said, "Let the little children come to me and do not hinder them, for to such belongs the kingdom of heaven" (Matt. 19:14 ESV). Furthermore, Paul teaches that the children of believing parents are not "unclean," but they "are holy" (1 Cor. 7:14).

Both traditions should be respected. However, those who baptize infants should make it very clear that the baptism is not finally effectual unless and until the child makes a personal profession of faith. Likewise, those who practice believers' baptism must remember that God honors and blesses the entire family into which they have entered as a whole.

Conclusion

All joyfully agree that baptism represents our formal, public entry into the Christian faith and into the community of the redeemed. We are not simply baptized by faith; we are baptized into a faith, i.e., into the blessed fellowship of all the redeemed. Whether we are Pentecostals or Baptists or Methodists, we should recognize our common inheritance as redeemed sinners who have been brought by the initiative of the triune God into the family of faith.

The Lord's Supper (Communion)

The Lord's Supper invites us into a deep mystery that can never be fully fathomed. However, as a basic primer, one way to start is to look at the Lord's Supper through three different lenses: past, present, and future.

Lens of the Past

The first thing to realize when you stand before the Lord's Supper is that there is a whole story of redemption represented in front of you that began long before you, or even your most distant ancestors, were ever born. We are stepping into the middle of something. It is a story that began before us, and it is a story that is still unfolding, until its final consummation. So, we cannot even begin to understand what we are stepping into until we first look back.

This "looking back" begins by remembering that God instituted the sacrament of the Lord's Supper at the Jewish Passover. The Passover meal was the annual commemoration of the Jews celebrating and remembering God's dramatic intervention in saving the children of Israel out of the bondage of Egyptian slavery. The Jews would partake of a meal that remembered and reenacted what God did that first Passover night when the blood of the lamb spared them from the judgment of death.

In the same way, when we take the Lord's Supper, we look back on our redemption from spiritual bondage. Jesus Christ inaugurated a new Passover. In Jesus Christ, God has, once again, intervened in human history. Through His incarnation, death on the cross, bodily resurrection, and ascension to the right hand of the Father, the powers of sin and death have been defeated. We look back and remember our own baptisms, and our own great redemption, and how God delivered us from bondage and brought us into His adoptive family. When we look back we see a great sequence of redemptive acts of which we are now a part.

Lens of the Present

The second lens through which we can capture something of the mystery of the Lord's Supper is the lens of the present. Communion is a celebration of the presence of Christ with His people today. We do not simply look back and remember what God once did. We celebrate the ongoing unfolding of His grand plan of redemption. Christ meets us at the Table today.

Christians have often discussed what happens when the minister stands up front and consecrates the elements of bread and wine in this sacred service. This seems to focus too much on the elements themselves, as if we are trying to find something magical or, at least, some mystery in the elements themselves. However, we can miss the main point, which is not the presence of the elements, but the promised presence of Christ at this Table. We should never miss the more profound transformation that occurs at the Lord's Table. It is the Lord's presence, not just the bread and wine, which transforms us as the people of God.

We are now part of this grand, unfolding story of God's redemption as we "feed upon Christ" and realize that we are not in this journey alone. We have one another, and Christ is present with us now. The one loaf reminds us that we are now part of the body of Christ. This is not a denominational belonging, or denominational "togetherness" per se, though we all need to be rooted in traditions that allow us to fully flourish. The foundation of all the fellowship and joy we have with one another is rooted and grounded in our common belonging to Christ; we are His body. We are Christians. By Christ's promised presence here, we are transformed anew by the His presence in the elements. Whenever Christ is present, everything is transformed. How can anything remain untransformed in the presence of Christ?

When Jesus rose from the dead, He appeared to His disciples for a period of forty days, and then He ascended to heaven, where He is seated at the right hand of the Father.

Jesus' ascension should not be seen as merely localizing Jesus in a particular place, meaning Jesus was *here* "on earth" and now He is *there* "in heaven." It is true, of course, that Jesus, through the ascension, is now seated at the right hand of God the Father Almighty in heaven. But in the ascension, Jesus also reassumed His omnipresence. This means that He is not only in heaven but, by His Spirit, He is present everywhere. You will recall that Jesus promised that "where two or three are gathered in my name, there am I among them" (Matt. 18:20 ESV). This was not possible during the incarnation, when His presence was localized. This is a promise that was fulfilled through the ascension.

This is important when we think about the Lord's Supper. Jesus is present at the Lord's Table. He promises to meet us. The Lord's Supper is the greatest example of meeting together in His name. When we eat the bread and drink the cup, we are mystically entering into the power of His death and resurrection. We recognize afresh that we are part of the redeemed community. This is a present reality, despite whatever we are going through in life. His body was broken for us. His blood was shed for us.

This raises another important issue. Should only baptized believers be invited forward to receive the Lord's Supper? All Christian traditions believe that the Lord's Supper is for believers, and that Scripture is clear that it is wrong to "eat or drink in an unworthy manner"

(1 Cor. 11:27), i.e., to receive the Lord's Supper in a casual or unreflective manner. However, not all agree that this, therefore, means that only Christians should be invited forward. Some traditions, such as Methodists, believe that the Lord's Supper can be a "converting ordinance."[1] This means that since Christ is truly present at the Table, then an unbeliever could come forward and receive Christ at the moment of his or her receiving the elements of the Lord's Supper.

Those who favor restricting the Table to those who have already been baptized, or even those who belong to that particular church or denomination, practice what is known as "fencing the Table." This means the pastor makes it clear that children, unbaptized adults or, in some cases, those who do not belong to that particular church or tradition, should refrain from coming forward.

Other traditions insist that since it is the Lord's Table, and not belonging to any particular denomination, we should not hinder God's work in the life of anyone when Christ is present at His table. Therefore, they practice what is known as "open Communion" and invite anyone who is repentant of his or her sins and prepared to trust in Christ to come forward and to partake. If an unbeliever receives Christ at the Table, then he or she would then be catechized into the faith, receive baptism, and be brought into the full fellowship and communion of the church.

Lens of the Future

Finally, Communion is a further way that the church proclaims the gospel to the world. The sacraments are very different from preaching. Preaching is the Word that goes forth and strikes the ears of the world and the believing community. Communion visibly demonstrates the gospel and is not just an *ear* witness, but an *eye* witness of the mystery of the gospel. It is not just something we say; it is something we do. We remind ourselves and the world that the kingdom has not yet fully come. We do not live in a perfect or perfectible world, but a fallen world. Our world is full of sin and fallenness, and we eagerly await the visible, bodily return of Christ. Paul himself testifies about this when he says in reference to the Lord's Supper, "For whenever you eat this bread and drink this cup, you proclaim the Lord's death until he comes" (1 Cor. 11:26).

The Lord's Supper is a proclamation of His death until His bodily return. Every time we share in the Lord's Supper, we do not only look back and remember our past redemption. We do not only receive Christ's forgiveness and grace as He walks with us right now, today. It is also a testimony to future realities. By faith we look to the culmination of this great story of redemption. Christ will return and fully inaugurate His kingdom. One of the high points of the Communion liturgy is when we say as a congregation, "Christ has died (past), Christ is risen (present), and Christ will come again (future)."

We look to that day when Christ will fully consummate His kingdom. We currently live in the tension between the "already" and the "not yet." Someday, all the enemies of Christ will be put under His feet and the kingdom of God will be fully realized. The Scriptures teach that the culmination of the ages and the inauguration of the kingdom will be accompanied by a great banquet, a feast with all of God's people through the ages, including Abraham, Isaac, and Jacob (Matt. 8:11; Rev. 19:9). This banquet will also include the thief on the cross and all of us sinners who, by grace, have received the good news of the kingdom. It is known as the marriage supper of the Lamb (Rev. 19:9 ESV), and it is the time when all the realities of the New Creation will be fully revealed. There will be new heavens and a new earth. All will be restored. The biggest transformation will be the absence of sin and the full manifestation of the eternal presence of Christ.

The elements of the Lord's Supper are actually connected to this larger feast at the end of time. You should see the elements of the Lord's Supper (bread and wine) as the hors d'oeuvres in anticipation of the larger feast which is to come. It is also a sign that the New Creation has already broken into the present order of life. For the Christian, we do not just wait for the glories of heaven to come, we are to live in anticipation of those realities in the present. The church should be a mini outpost of those realities. The church (whether meeting together on Sunday morning, or as we are scattered around society throughout the week) should be a visible sign of radical grace, joyful forgiveness, bold justice, and sacrificial love. In the midst of a world that is preoccupied with the smaller narratives of war in Afghanistan, the latest Hollywood film, or the rise and fall of the stock market, we should be the living testimony of a greater, grander narrative that is unfolding in the world: namely, the glorious redemption of sinners who are being adopted by God and brought under His loving rule and reign.

Conclusion

All of these realities—past, present, and future—are brought together when we celebrate the Lord's Supper. As I noted at the outset, the mysteries of the Lord's Supper are great, indeed. This is merely a brief primer to introduce you to a lifetime journey that draws you deeper and deeper into this great mystery which is only fully known and understood in the presence of Christ Himself.

PART III

The Lord's Prayer

Introduction

In our overview of the Ten Commandments, we discovered that this code does not exhaust the moral life of God, but serves as a broad framework for the whole law and as a pointer to the depths of sanctification, which only the triune God embodies and can lead us to. In the same way, the Lord's Prayer should not be seen as a prayer we memorize and mumble out in some rote fashion, but as a pattern for a life of prayer and contemplative meditation in the presence of God. The reason the Lord's Prayer appears in catechesis guides across the centuries is twofold. First, it is because the moral framework of the Ten Commandments (especially as deepened in the Sermon on the Mount) compels us to prayer, which acknowledges our need for the enabling presence of God. Second, the Lord's Prayer is the paradigm for all prayer, including set liturgical prayers as well as the kind of spontaneous prayers we might pray that are known only to God. The Lord's Prayer gives us the basic "grammar" of all prayer.

The overall structure of the Lord's Prayer is similar to what we observed with the Ten Commandments. The Decalogue is, broadly speaking, divided between our moral obligations to God (commandments 1–4) and our moral obligations to our neighbor (commandments 5–10). In the same way the Lord's Prayer is made up of five main phrases or petitions. The first two are clearly related to our life before God and His work in the world. The latter three give us the proper orientation toward ourselves and our neighbors. This brief overview of the Lord's Prayer is designed to point out the significance of the five phrases and how it serves as the foundation for our entire life of prayer.

Just as the Ten Commandments are found in two locations in the Old Testament (Exodus 20 and Deuteronomy 5), so the Lord's Prayer is found in two locations in the New Testament. It is found in Matthew 6:9–13 as a part of the Sermon on the Mount (Matthew 5–7) and it is found in Luke 11:2–4 as a part of Jesus' teaching on prayer. In Luke's gospel the prayer is given to us in an abbreviated form. But in both versions the same five phrases or petitions are found. Here are the two prayers as they appear in Matthew and Luke:

Matthew 6:9–13	Luke 11:2–4
Our Father in heaven, hallowed be your name,	Father, hallowed be your name,
Your kingdom come, your will be done on earth as it is in heaven.	Your kingdom come.
Give us today our daily bread.	Give us each day our daily bread.
Forgive us our debts, as we also have forgiven our debtors.	Forgive us our sins, for we also forgive everyone who sins against us.
And lead us not into temptation, but deliver us from the evil one.	And lead us not into temptation.

A brief examination of the overall structure reveals that the first two phrases focus on God and His name, His kingdom, and His will. The final three phrases focus on our bread, our sins, and our temptations. Even this most basic observation has the potential to dramatically change our prayer life. If we think of our prayers (especially our more informal, spontaneous prayers), they almost always focus on our needs and the challenges we have with those around us. If we have time, we might pray about and think about God and His name, glory, will, and kingdom. Thus, from the outset, the Lord's Prayer calls for a radical reorientation of our prayer lives, putting God's glory before our needs.

You may also notice that when the Lord's Prayer is publicly prayed in church, it often includes the final phrase: "For yours is the kingdom, and the power, and the glory forever. Amen." This final phrase is not found in the original teachings of Jesus, but was liturgically added by the early church to assist the church in seeing the kingdom framework of the entire prayer. Since it is not always possible to point out to congregations week after week the kingdom orientation of the overall prayer, it was probably wise that this phrase was added to the prayer when it was prayed publicly. However, this guide will only focus on each of the five phrases found in the original teachings of Jesus. It is to these that we now turn.

PETITION 1

Our Father in heaven, hallowed be your name

Our Father ...

At the very threshold of the Lord's Prayer, in Matthew 6:9, we find a glorious revelation unmatched in the religious history of the world, and known to us only by divine self-disclosure. The two words "Our Father" usher us into a vibrant relationship with God. We pray not as slaves seeking to hear and obey a powerful master, but as children who have been graciously ushered into the joyous presence of their father. We come not as lone and isolated searchers after God, but as a part of the great communion of the saints. It is not "My Master," or even "My Father," but "Our Father." We are brought into the joyful presence of both the Trinity (of which Jesus and the Spirit also join in by saying, "Our Father") and all the company of the redeemed. We should not miss the fact that the phrase "Our Father" simultaneously implies both the doctrine of the Trinity and the doctrine of the communion of the saints. We, as the people of God, are brought up into the fellowship which heretofore has only been enjoyed in the mysteries of God's own triune life.

. . . in heaven

We pray from the limited frame and perspective of earth-bound space and time. However, God dwells in heaven. He is outside of time. He sees the end from the beginning. When we pray, we enter into His presence, knowing that we are thereby entering into His perspective and lordship over all of time and history. He is on the throne of the universe; we are not. This phrase reminds us that we are submitting our perspective to His perfect wisdom, right at the outset of our prayer. So often what we call "unanswered prayers" have actually been answered from the perspective of heaven, but we have failed to discern the answer because it came to us in an unexpected way.

Hallowed be your name

Earlier, in our discussion on the third commandment, I pointed out that to call upon someone's name is to call upon the character of that person and the associated power identified with him or her. So, when we say, as the New American Standard Bible puts it, "Our Father, who is in heaven, hallowed be your name," we are acknowledging the holiness and the sacredness of His name.

I noted earlier that the Bible gives God many names, and listed quite a few. However, all of those names are summarized by one title: holy. The word *hallowed* means "holy." It is not that there is a hierarchy of names, with ones like "Lion of the Tribe of Judah" and "Judge" near the bottom, and names like "Lamb of God" and "Savior" a bit higher, and finally, "Holy" at the top. God's character qualities cannot be ranked like that, because He bears all of them in their perfected state and in perfect harmony with all the others. Rather, the name "Holy" should be seen as containing all of God's other qualities and characteristics within the one affirmation. Thus, when we pray, "Holy is your name," we are, in that one phrase, confessing all of God's nature and character in the single word!

Interestingly, of all the names and titles attributed to God, only "holy" appears in triplicate form. It is known as the Trisagion, meaning "triple holy," and appears in this form twice in the Bible. It first appears in Isaiah 6 when the prophet has his vision of heaven and sees the six winged seraphs flying around the throne and crying out day and night, "Holy, holy, holy" (vv. 2–3). The threefold "holy" appears again in John's vision of heaven in Revelation. He also sees "six winged creatures" who cry out day and night, "Holy, holy, holy" (Rev. 4:8).[1]

It is significant that both the Ten Commandments and the Lord's Prayer have this wonderful convergence in protecting and honoring the holiness of God's name. This is the foundation for all prayer and, indeed, our entire relationship with God. When Moses first encountered God at the burning bush, he was told to take off his shoes, for he was on holy ground (Exod. 3:5). Likewise, when we first learn to pray and come into God's presence, we begin by recognizing that we are on holy ground. All our prayers and our hopes, and even our darkest pain, must ultimately pass through the sanctifying fires of His holiness.

Your kingdom come, your will be done on earth as it is in heaven

Your kingdom come

When we think about the word *kingdom*, our mind quickly goes to faraway images associated more with medieval Europe than with the world in which we live. Therefore, it is important at the outset to understand what the word *kingdom* means. It does not primarily refer to a geographical place, such as the United Kingdom or the Kingdom of Saudi Arabia. It also should not be understood to refer to any particular political party or plan. In the Bible the kingdom of God is more about God's reign than a particular geographic realm or governance plan. The kingdom of God is about God's kingly reign. God is the King. He rules and reigns over all.

When Jesus teaches us to pray that God's kingdom would come, it is a prayer that the rule of God would be fully known and established in the church, in our lives, and throughout the world. It transcends every country or political system because it sits in judgment over them all and, in the end, will triumph over them all. In the book of Revelation, Jesus is given the name "KING OF KINGS AND LORD OF LORDS" (19:16). This is the heart of the kingdom of God: Jesus Christ is Lord! To pray for God's kingdom to come is an acknowledgment that the rule and reign of God is coming and so we are praying for the hastening of that day, and that we would be fully in harmony with God's reign as it is breaking into the present order.

Your will be done on earth as it is in heaven

There is a great gulf between the rule and reign of God in heaven and the rule and reign of God on earth. In heaven, God's sovereignty is fully known and acknowledged. In heaven, there is no sin, injustice, or any deviation from God's glorious rule and reign. On earth, God's rule is only seen in distorted, fragmented ways. When we pray for God's will to be done on earth as it is in heaven, we are longing for the day when the reality of God's rule that is already present in heaven would fully manifest itself in the earth. In the incarnation of God in Jesus Christ, we were able to see up close the rule and reign of God fully present in Him.

In Jesus Christ the rule of God was inaugurated into the world in a fresh way. The first words of Jesus in His public ministry were, "The time has come. The kingdom of God is near. Repent and believe the good news!" (Mark 1:15). It is the announcement of the great invasion of God's rule into the broken, fallen world of sin and death. God's rule reverses the power of sin and overturns death itself. All through Jesus' ministry we hear Him speaking of the kingdom of God, declaring in word and deed that the in-breaking of God's rule has finally come.

Every gathering of believers around the world should be seen as a little outpost of the kingdom of God. The church is to be the living example of God's rule and reign in the world. The kingdom of God is, therefore, being dynamically revealed in history as His reign and rule extends through the preaching of the gospel and the empowerment of the Holy Spirit. In the church and in the lives of Christians, we should see the realities of heaven made fully manifest. The world may be full of deceit and greed, but it should never be so in the church. The world may be full of evil and injustice, but it should never be so in the church.

This is why it is so embarrassing when scandals break out in the church or in the lives of Christians. It discredits the very foundation upon which the church stands, namely, that it is an outpost of the rule and reign of God. This is also why it is so important for such scandals, when they do occur, to be swiftly acknowledged and repented of, so that "God's name [will not be] blasphemed among the Gentiles because of you" (Rom. 2:24).

This is why we daily pray that God's rule and reign would come and that the gap between His rule in heaven and His rule on earth would become narrower. When we fight for justice, we help narrow the gap. When we stand against evil, we help narrow the gap. This process continues until Jesus comes and fully consummates His kingdom, judges the world, defeats all demonic powers, vindicates His children, and fully ushers in the New Creation, where God's rule and reign are without end. We do not know the exact process through which God's dominion will finally be manifest. We only know that the last enemy of God that will be destroyed will be death itself: "For he must reign until he has put all his enemies under his feet. The last enemy to be destroyed is death" (1 Cor. 15:25–26).

PETITION 3

Give us today our daily bread

This is the point in the Lord's Prayer when we transition from our prayers related to God's holiness, His will, and His kingdom, to our own needs. There is nothing wrong with a prayer that contains the word "give," but we should not start our prayers this way. Before we ask God to give us something, we must first orient ourselves to Him and His rule and reign. This is why the Lord's Prayer is the model prayer. It reminds us to first orient ourselves to Him. The Scriptures say, "Enter his gates with thanksgiving and his courts with praise" (Ps. 100:4). It does not say, "Enter his presence with petitions and his courts with requests." However, once we properly orient ourselves to His rule and reign, then we are invited to ask God to meet our specific needs.

As a model prayer, the phrase "our daily bread" has two important features on which we should focus. First, the word "bread" as it is used in this prayer symbolizes all of our basic needs. In ancient Israel, as in many parts of the world even today, bread was the staple of life. If Jesus' ministry had been in South India or in China, He might have said, "Give us our daily bowl of rice." The point is that "bread" represents our daily needs. By extension, the phrase reaches beyond food and would include everything we need for daily life, including food, clothing, housing, honest government, health, family, and friends, to name just a few.

The second, and equally important, feature of the phrase "our daily bread" is the force that lies behind the word "daily." Notice that when God promises to meet our needs, it is a *daily* promise. In the days of the wilderness wanderings, the manna was provided daily. No manna was to be hoarded for future weeks (Exod. 16:13–33). It is an early example of God teaching His people about daily dependence upon Him. While the word "bread" encompasses everything we need in this life, it does not always come in advance installments. Many of us have sufficient provisions for our lives for months, or even years, in advance. This is a great blessing from God, but it can lead us to a lower awareness of our daily dependence upon God for everything we need.

The Scriptures give us a picture of two people with barns that are filled. The first picture is the righteous man of Psalm 144. He has a barn "filled with every kind of provision." The picture is one of abundance. His "sheep will increase by thousands" (v. 13). His "oxen will draw heavy loads" (v. 14). How blessed is the one "of whom this is true" (v. 15).

The second picture is the rich fool of Luke 12. His barns are also full of grain and goods. He had such an abundant crop that he had no place to store all of his grain. So, he decides to tear down his barns and build bigger ones. He then says to himself, "You have plenty of good things laid up for many years. Take life easy; eat, drink and be merry" (v. 19). But, unlike the righteous man of Psalm 144, this man is called a "fool" by God because he didn't realize that God was the source of his life. In fact, he did not realize that on that very night he was going to die (v. 20).

These two pictures reveal the importance of trusting God daily for our provisions and being generous with what we have. It may very well be that our abundance may be today's daily source for us as well as our neighbor in need.

PETITION 4

Forgive us our debts, as we also have forgiven our debtors

Forgive us our debts . . .

The fourth petition of the Lord's Prayer acknowledges that we stand as sinners before God and are in need of His forgiveness.[1] *Sin* refers to anything that contradicts, or is inconsistent with, God's holiness, and thereby creates a breach in the relationship between ourselves and God. The Scriptures teach that sin is far more than merely the mistakes we make or even our violations of the Ten Commandments outlined in this study. Sin is the breaking of a divine relationship.

The Scriptures also teach that there is no one without sin. This is taught in both the Old and the New Testaments. For example, in 1 Kings 8 we have recorded Solomon's prayer of dedication for the temple. In the prayer, Solomon makes nine references to our sin, including the phrase "for there is no one who does not sin" (v. 46). Likewise, the New Testament teaches that "all have sinned and fall[en] short of the glory of God" (Rom. 3:23). Because sin is not merely a matter of outward actions, but of the disposition of our hearts, there is no one who is without sin. Therefore, the entire human race stands in a broken relationship with God. There are no exceptions.

To make matters worse, there is nothing we can do to restore the relationship since we are so thoroughly oriented to resist God's will. It is a debt we cannot pay. In fact, Paul says that we are "dead in our trespasses and sins" (Eph. 2:1, 5; Col. 2:13). Dead people are powerless to help themselves. No amount of good works can heal the breach.

Hindus travel hundreds of miles to dip in the Ganges river, but it has no power to heal this relationship. Muslims pray every day, fast for a month each year, and even make a pilgrimage to Mecca, but none of these things have the power to take away sins. God alone must act on our behalf. The good news of the gospel is that this is precisely what God has done by sending His Son into the world to die on the cross for our sins.

In the Lord's Prayer, we ask God to forgive us our debts because it is something only He can do. We ask not on the basis of anything we have done, but by casting ourselves on God's mercy and trusting in the provision that has been made for us in Jesus Christ. Paul says, "When you were dead in your sins . . . God made you alive with Christ. He forgave us all our sins, having cancelled the written code, with its regulations, that was against us and that stood opposed to us; he took it away, nailing it to the cross" (Col. 2:13–14). This is our justification. But asking God to forgive us is also an ongoing, daily rhythm in our lives as we increasingly become aware of the great gulf between His holiness and our sinfulness.

. . . *as we also have forgiven our debtors*

This part of the petition brings two very important truths to light. First, we see that the good news of the gospel is not an expression of cheap grace. In other words, God's forgiveness is not merely granted in isolation from the larger network of our relationships and our own grateful response to God's grace. We are saved and ushered into the community of God's redeemed people. We cannot and should not pretend that this is not so. Therefore, God's forgiveness is linked to our forgiving those who have sinned against us. In short, the vertical act of God's forgiveness in the Lord's Prayer is dynamically linked to the horizontal act of forgiving others.

This teaching is so radical and so disturbing to our way of living and thinking that Jesus reinforced and restated it immediately after He taught His disciples the Lord's Prayer. The prayer as it appears in Matthew 6:9–13 is immediately followed with the teaching: "For if you forgive men when they sin against you, your heavenly father will also forgive you.

But if you do not forgive men their sins, your Father will not forgive your sins" (Matt. 6:14–15; see also Matthew 18:15–35).

God's plan is not merely to reconcile people to Himself, but to reconcile the whole human race to one another. Paul says, "If anyone is in Christ, he [or she] is a new creation. The old has passed away; behold, the new has come. All this is from God, who through Christ reconciled us to himself and gave us the ministry of reconciliation" (2 Cor. 5:17–18 ESV). We are reconciled that we might become ministers of reconciliation. We know that we have truly heard and received the good news of God's forgiveness when we respond by forgiving others. Likewise, if we refuse to forgive those who have hurt us in some way, then we must not have ever really received the good news of God's grace, and we remain unreconciled to God. In short, God will not be reconciled to us if we refuse to be reconciled to our neighbor.

The second truth, which is related to the first, is the use of the word "we." This reinforces the point that we should not overly privatize this prayer or, for that matter, the Christian faith as a whole. It is true that, through faith, we are personally reconciled to God. However, the gospel is never content to remain purely a private affair, or just a matter of our own hearts before God. It may never be less than that, but it is certainly a great deal more than that. The Lord's Prayer points us to the deeper realization that the work of reconciliation includes an ever-widening circle of people whom God is calling to Himself. We may be justified as individuals, but the work of sanctification inevitably brings us into community, and in the end, our final glorification occurs as joyful members of the body and bride of Christ.

PETITION 5

And lead us not into temptation, but deliver us from the evil one

The fifth and final petition of the Lord's Prayer recalls the great cosmic battle of which we are a part. The true nature of this conflict is only slowly revealed in the Scripture. Beginning in the early part of the Old Testament, known as the Pentateuch (Genesis–Deuteronomy), God revealed to us that there were two paths: the way of blessing and the way of curse; the way of life and the way of death. We were called to choose which path we would follow (see Deuteronomy 27:14–26; 28:1–68; 30:19–20).

In the psalms we are shown that there are two ways, the way of the righteous and the way of the wicked. This structure and tension is embedded into almost all of the psalms, but is best exemplified by Psalm 1, which pictures the righteous as a tree planted by streams of water, and the wicked as the chaff which the wind blows away.

In the book of Proverbs, this tension is expressed in terms of the wise and the foolish. This theme dominates the whole of Proverbs and is perhaps best stated in the very first proverb, which portrays the wise as the one who fears God, and the foolish as one who despises wisdom and shuns discipline (Prov. 1:7).

In the Old Testament, the prophets also describe these same two paths, but use the language of the covenant to express it. There are those who obey God and keep the covenant and those who rebel against God and reject the covenant. The entire Old Testament lays the foundation for this massive struggle, which permeates the whole of life. There is the path of blessing, righteousness, wisdom, and obedience; and there is the path of curse, wickedness, foolishness, and rebellion.

Jesus reinforces this theme in the Sermon on the Mount when He speaks about two ways: the wide gate and the broad road, which leads to destruction; and the small gate and narrow road, which leads to life. Many follow the former, but few find the latter (Matt. 7:13–14).

However, it is in the Lord's Prayer that we fully recognize that this struggle is both personal and cosmic. It is not merely a struggle against evil, but the evil one, i.e., the devil, or Satan. It is not merely a human struggle against "flesh and blood," but a struggle against "principalities and power" (RHE) and the "spiritual forces of evil in the heavenly realms" (Eph. 6:12).

It is in the New Testament that we fully realize that behind all of the foolish, rebellious, wicked actions in the world stands Satan, who seeks to set up his own diabolical kingdom in contrast to the kingdom of God. It is in the New Testament that we see demons challenging the Son of God, not just the rebellious wicked world in opposition to Him.

In the Lord's Prayer we pray that we might be delivered from the evil one. Some translations, and frequently in churches when the Lord's Prayer is cited, it is stated as "deliver us from evil" rather than "deliver us from the evil one." However, it is important to recognize that even when we say "evil," we must realize that Satan stands behind all the evil in the world and that this pseudo-reign is far more than the aggregate accumulation of all the various acts of evil in the world.

It was important to start with the second phrase of this final petition to establish the larger context of evil. However, the first phrase raises a very important, if not troubling, question: Does God lead us into temptation? It is a question that does not have an easy answer. If He does lead us into temptation, then why does He do it? If He does not lead us into temptation, then why does He instruct us to pray that He won't?

James teaches that "when tempted, no one should say, 'God is tempting me.' For God cannot be tempted by evil, nor does he tempt anyone; but each one is tempted when, by his own evil desire, he is dragged away and enticed" (James 1:13–14). This clearly establishes that God is not the tempter. Satan is the tempter, and we are also carried along by our own evil desires within us.

However, it is important to remember that, unlike Zoroastrianism, Christianity does not believe in two *equal* cosmic powers, one good and one evil. Rather, the Bible affirms that God is sovereign over all, including the evil one. This phrase of the Lord's Prayer is an acknowledgment of God's sovereignty over everything. Satan was defeated by God at the cross, and the full ramifications of that victory are slowly unfolding according to God's time and God's plan. At the end of time, Satan will be cast into the lake of fire (Rev. 20:10) and God's triumph will be fully consummated and manifest for all to see. So, asking God to not "lead us into temptation" acknowledges God's ultimate sovereignty over all things.

God is faithful in both walking with us through the fiery trials of life and, in other cases, delivering us from the fiery trial altogether. Why we are sometimes asked to walk through the dark valleys of pain, suffering, and temptation, and other times we are powerfully protected from all of the same, is a matter of the mystery of God's sovereign work and plan. It calls for humility and trust, both of which are certainly among the great undergirding themes of all prayer, especially the Lord's Prayer.

Amen

Although the text does not end with the word *amen*, this is such a widespread practice in prayers across the world, it may be worth noting something about it. First of all, the word appears in both the Old and New Testaments and carries the meaning of "so be it" or "let it be so." It is used at the end of prayers (e.g., 1 Chron. 16:36; Eph. 3:20–21) as a final sign of God's sovereignty in our prayers.

The etymology of the word *amen* is not certain. It is worth noting that the root of the Hebrew word for *amen* is the same as the word for *faith* (āmēn / 'āmán). Thus, when we say, "So be it," we are trusting God in faith, not simply acquiescing to fatalism. Furthermore, an ancient rabbinical teaching manual, known as the Talmud, says that the word is an acronym for the phrase "God is a trustworthy King."

To say, "amen," at the end of this or any other prayer is to acknowledge God's sovereignty and, in effect, to give God full and complete editing rights to your prayers. For example, you may be praying earnestly for God to give you a particular job you have applied for. God hears your prayer, but He knows that He has a better job waiting for you that you do not yet know about. So, you are praying, quite literally, "Lord, please give me this job," and after the "Amen," God edits your prayers to say, "Lord, please do not give me this job." God answers the prayer, which we, at the moment, see as an unanswered prayer but, later on, see God's editorial work with fuller appreciation and gratitude. It has been observed that in prayer, we often ask for Band-Aids, when God knows we need major surgery. These are simple examples, but it does reveal something about the grand complexity of prayer when a finite being with limited knowledge and perspective is praying to the eternal Lord and God of the universe!

Conclusion

We have examined each of the phrases of the Lord's Prayer. However, we began by stating that the Lord's Prayer is the model for all prayer. It provides, as it were, the "grammar" for all prayer. Therefore, in conclusion, let's step back and take a sweeping look at the Lord's Prayer as a whole.

It may be helpful to see the Lord's Prayer as a great drama of divine-human discourse that unfolds in three acts. Act 1 is the Holiness of God. The whole prayer, as we observed, begins with an acknowledgment of God's holy name. Act 2, at the heart of the prayer, is the Love of God. Here we meet the God who loves us, cares for us, and is prepared to meet our daily needs. Act 3 is the Sovereignty of God, the One in whom we must trust and upon whom we rely, even in the face of what looks like "unanswered" prayer or situations that make us wonder if God is really in control.

If we emphasize the love of God without the larger context of His holiness and His sovereignty, we end up drifting into mere sentimentality. If we emphasize holiness and sovereignty without the love of God, then it can all too easily drift toward a God who is powerful, but aloof and distant. The Lord's Prayer provides the perfect frame of holiness, love, and sovereignty, a little mini-drama which serves to enliven all of our prayers.

Final Thoughts

These reflections on the Ten Commandments, the two sacraments, and the Lord's Prayer bring to a conclusion this introduction to some of the core practices of the Christian faith. Working together they serve to unite all Christians around the world and back through time. They represent only the beginning of a lifetime of study and reflection on the great mystery of Christian identity. It is hoped that those who complete this study will be deeply moved as they consider what a great salvation is ours through the work of the triune God.

Notes

Part I

Commandment 2

1. Pope Francis, *Lumen Fidei*, Encyclical Letter #1 (Rome: June 29, 2013), 16.

Commandment 6

1. The Hebrew phrase "Lo tirtsach" (can be transliterated *tirtsach* or *tirtzach*) means "Do not murder." The King James Bible mistranslated the phrase as "Do not kill."

Commandment 9

1. If the testifying person does not believe in or has a religious conviction against taking oaths, then courts accept a substitution of the phrase "so help you God" with the phrase "under pains and penalties of perjury." The former is an "oath," the latter is an "affirmation," but both carry the same legal force.

Commandment 10

1. This quote is commonly attributed to John Bunyan, however there is some question about its actual source. For more information see http://thegospelcoalition.org/blogs/justintaylor/2011/07/27/run-john-run/.

Part II

Introduction

1. *Book of Common Prayer* (Athens, GA: Anglican Parishes Association, 1928).

Baptism

1. There are certain situations under extreme persecution where this public act may not be possible, but may need to be done in a more private setting. However, this should be seen as the exception to the rule, rather than the normative way in which a new believer receives baptism.

2. There are a few Christian groups who do not baptize, such as Quakers and the Salvation Army. However, this is a minority position in the church. The Salvation Army, for example, is not theologically opposed to the sacraments per se. Rather, at some point they felt that the outward signs (baptism and Lord's Supper) had eclipsed the spiritual meaning and had become such a dead ritual for so many that the only way to recapture the original spiritual nature of conversion was to emphasize the inner truth, not the outward forms.

The Lord's Supper

1. *Book of Common Prayer* (Athens, GA: Anglican Parishes Association, 1928), 581.

Part III

Petition 1

1. Some also include Psalm 99, the overall structure of which has a threefold "holy" (vv. 3, 5, 9).

Petition 4

1. Some Christian traditions use the word "trespasses," whereas others use "debts." Both words are used to speak about the weight of sin that is upon us.

About the Author

Dr. Timothy Tennent received his M.Div. in 1984 from Gordon-Conwell; the Th.M. in Ecumenics, with a focus on Islam, from Princeton Theological Seminary; and did graduate work in linguistics (TESL) at the University of Georgia. He completed his Ph.D. in Non-western Christianity with a focus on Hinduism and Indian Christianity in 1998 at the University of Edinburgh in Scotland. He served eleven years as professor of World Missions and Indian Studies at Gordon-Conwell Theological Seminary in South Hamilton, Massachusetts. He has ministered and taught in China, Thailand, Nigeria, Eastern Europe, and India. Ordained in the United Methodist Church, he has pastored churches throughout the country.

In 2009, Dr. Tennent was inaugurated as the eighth president of Asbury Theological Seminary. In addition to his service as president of the seminary and professor of World

Christianity, he is author to a growing collection of books and publications on missions and global Christianity. He also serves on the faculty of Luther W. New Jr. Theological College of Dehra Dun, India, where he has taught annually since 1989.

Visit TimothyTennent.com to follow Dr. Tennent's blog, listen to his sermons, and further connect with his work. Follow him on Twitter @timtennent.